A Pocket Guide to Suffering

Mike Abendroth

COPYRIGHT @ 2024 NOCO MEDIA

All rights reserved. No part of this book may be reproduced in any form without written permission from the publisher and author.

All Scripture quotations are from The ESV® Bible (The Holy Bible, English Standard Version®), © 2001 by Crossway, a publishing ministry of Good News Publishers. Used by permission. All rights reserved.

PURPOSE

The purpose of this book is simple: to direct the attention of all suffering Christians to Jesus Christ. While the title of the book includes the word "cancer," the truths in this book will help any Christian who has any type of physical affliction, sickness or trial.

INTRODUCTION: MY STORY

Cancer #1

December 2015. Christmas is around the corner. My children at university would all be home for the holidays. My PSA test (to measure possible prostate cancer) spiked. After some consultation, twelve biopsies were extracted. While I am sure birthing a baby hurts more, and broken femurs are worse, twelve prostate biopsies (plus the lidocaine injection) must be a close third on the pain scale. I gripped the exam table so hard that my hand hurt, and I lost count of the biopsies. The doctor said he would call with the results.

I had just finished a two-hour radio show which was both exhilarating and stressful. After it was finished, I walked over to my desk and saw my phone indicating a voicemail. I braced myself. I pressed, "voicemail." "Hi Mike, this is Doctor _____, please call me when you get an opportunity." At that very moment, I knew I had prostate cancer. Why? If I did not have cancer, the voicemail would have gone this way: "Hi Mike, this is Doctor _____, the tests came back negative. If you want to know the details, call me at your convenience. Have a Merry Christmas."

One and a half years later, I had radiation (brachy therapy) on my prostate in a New York City hospital known for that prostate cancer treatment. Thankfully, everything went well, and I am prostate cancer free as of November 2024. My checkups are every twelve months.

Cancer #2

I must honestly say, the second time a physician tells you that you have cancer, it is easier than the first. The first time is shocking. The second time is, well, met more with resignation. After some bad blood tests, the diagnosis I received was leukemia. After further tests, bone biopsies, cardiology visits—all designed to make sure my body would be ready for "the treatment," or "the protocol" to kill chronic lymphocytic leukemia (CLL), I then started two oral drugs. The treatment will last anywhere from 12–24 months. As I write this book in late 2024, things are going according to schedule and the outlook is good. Besides some side effects (tiredness, headaches, lethargy, weight gain, GI issues, and a few others), I still work and try to exercise when I can.

The Routine

The first time you enter a cancer hospital for treatment is hard to forget. Everything seems new and strange. Bald people. Sick children. Wheelchairs.

Masks. Gray skin. Ports. IVs. Wristbands. Then the routine:

- Remember you parked on level P5
- Check in on the first floor
- Blood draw/IV insertion on the second floor
- Coffee and maybe some breakfast on the third floor (waiting for the blood results)
- Vital signs taken on the seventh floor
- Meet with the "Care Team" to go over symptoms, strategies, and procedures
- Receive infusions (if needed)
- Go to the pharmacy on the second floor
- And often, come back tomorrow

But back to the waiting room in the lab/blood draw area. The patients are easy to spot and not just because they look thin, bald, or sick. It is because they have a wristband for identification and a small, clip-on "locator." I first thought it was a Geiger counter or some radiation detection unit.

It is rare to see someone alone in the blood draw area, or for that matter, anywhere in the hospital. Most every patient is accompanied by a loved one or sometimes, a driver/helper. I have been driven to tears as I observe a supportive spouse gently rub the hand of their loved one, surely wondering what will happen next. And what will happen in the years to come, assuming they will both be around to experience them together. While I cannot read their minds, their faces seem full of perplexity, sorrow, surprise, and a certain quietness that is hard to quantify. The common denominator with most is that they look scared. They look like sheep without a shepherd. They need Jesus, the Chief Shepherd, the Good Shepherd and the Great Shepherd.

Thankfully, for every person who believes on the Lord Jesus Christ, this statement is true: cancer is not your shepherd. Cancer is not in charge. Cancer is not all powerful. Cancer does not have the last word. Cancer is not a surprise to the Lord. Cancer is not your shepherd.

Psalm 23
A Psalm of David.

The LORD is my shepherd; I shall not want.
He makes me lie down in green pastures.
He leads me beside still waters.
He restores my soul.
He leads me in paths of righteousness
for his name's sake.

Even though I walk through the valley
of the shadow of death,
I will fear no evil,
for you are with me;
your rod and your staff,

they comfort me.

You prepare a table before me
in the presence of my enemies;
you anoint my head with oil;
my cup overflows.
Surely goodness and mercy shall follow me
all the days of my life,
and I shall dwell in the house of the Lord forever.

John 10:11, 15, 17–18

"I am the good shepherd. The good shepherd lays down his life for the sheep. Just as the Father knows me and I know the Father; and I lay down my life for the sheep. For this reason the Father loves me, because I lay down my life that I may take it up again. No one takes it from me, but I lay it down of my own accord. I have authority to lay it down, and I have authority to take it up again. This charge I have received from my Father."

To repeat: suffering Christian, cancer is not your shepherd. You are not alone. You do not have to go through cancer treatments by yourself. While your family is surely super supportive, there is a friend who sticks closer than a brother, or spouse, or child. Jesus laid down His life for you. Jesus loves you. He will care for you. He will protect you. He will guide you. He will lead you. He will never leave you or forsake you. Jesus will not let you perish. You can trust Jesus for your eternal destiny and life. You are, by God's grace, in the safe hands of the Father.

One hospital visit, I said to my very supportive wife, "These people look like sheep without a shepherd." Certainly, some of the people I watch must be Christians, but many are not. I feel so bad for people who are going through such extreme trials, but they are going through them alone. They have turned their noses and backs on the Lord Jesus. They simply will not believe Him. Sin has blinded them. Seeing the lost, I desired to go into "pastor" or "chaplain" mode and simply walk up to each patient and say, "I am a pastor, can I read some of the Bible for you and then pray for you?" I want to point them to the Lord God, the One who shepherds, guides, protects, and cares for His sheep.

Like it or not, you are shepherded by something or someone. Everyone follows. Each person is led. You might be followed by time, circumstances, a worldview, debt, thoughts, illness, or a person. As pastor David Gibson writes, "We are each following someone or something all the time; we're relying on someone or something other than ourselves to keep us safe and protect us and to provide the comfort we need to face life unafraid."[1] Cancer shepherds because it

---

[1] David Gibson, *The Lord of Psalm 23*, (Wheaton: Crossway, 2023), 12.

leads. It directs. But sadly, it does not protect and provide. Cancer is a bad shepherd.

For unbelievers, the news gets worse before it gets better. The ultimate shepherd for people who are not Christians is death. Yes, death. The Psalmist pens these haunting words,

> *"Like sheep they are appointed for Sheol; death shall be their shepherd, and the upright shall rule over them in the morning. Their form shall be consumed in Sheol, with no place to dwell." (Psalm 49:14)*

If you are not a Christian, death is the ultimate terror, and it is inevitable. Your only hope to be rescued from the punishment of your own sin is to run, by faith, to the Lord Jesus Christ. The eternal Son took on flesh and dwelt among us. Jesus perfectly obeyed God's righteous laws entirely. He merited, or earned, righteousness and bestows it on all who believe in Him. Not only that, Jesus died a sinner's death, even though He was sinless, so that the just penalty for sin could be paid in full. To prove His victory over sin, Jesus raised Himself from the dead. All who call upon the name of the Lord shall be saved. Call on Him today.

And remember dear believer, cancer is not your shepherd.

CHAPTER 1
"YOU HAVE CANCER"

For about a year and a half, the first thing that entered my mind when I woke up was not, "Good morning, Lord." It was, "I have cancer." That thought sadly dominated my thinking throughout the day and for many months, even years. How do you stop thinking about your cancer?

Dear Christian, you who are struggling with cancer, your identity is not cancer. Do not read over this too rapidly. Your identity is not cancer. While you have cancer, it does not define you. As you know, your identity includes being a spouse, parent, sibling, friend, neighbor, co-worker. Yet there is something more foundational. Your identity is found in your Savior. You are a Christian, a child of the living God. To use the Apostle Paul's language, you are "in Christ."

How does God see you? Does He view you as a person with cancer, or a blood-bought son or daughter, all due to the great work of His Son, the risen Savior? You are not only made in God's likeness and image, but more than that, your Representative, Jesus, has united you to Himself.

I have heard it said that to have your identity in Christ is to proclaim that the most essential thing about yourself and it has zero to do with what you have personally done. Paul declares in Galatians 2:20, "I have been crucified with Christ. It is no longer I who live, but Christ who lives in me. And the life I now live in the flesh I live by faith in the Son of God, who loved me and gave himself for me." And it is true not just for Paul, but for every believer. Including believers with cancer.

Your significance is not what you do or do not do, nor is it in what you have done. Your identity is not found in cancer. You are a Christian. Now, go set your alarm for an early wake up call.

CHAPTER 2
HEBREWS AND CANCER

Before my first cancer diagnosis in 2015, I would say that there was no flagrant or disqualifying sin in my life. But what cancer did expose was deep-seated issues that are hard to root out and difficult to notice. Self-righteousness. Pride. Worry. Anxiety. Did I mention self-righteousness? And more. These sins were always there, regularly popping out, lurking and simmering, but cancer seemed to be the great revealer. In front of my family and the church, I put on a courageous face. And to the Lord's glory, there were times I walked by faith. The problem surfaced at nighttime, like a nightmare. The family slept and I worried. I googled. I cried. I borrowed trouble by becoming anxious about the future.

Because of cancer, I had come face-to-face with my spiritual inadequacies. I realized my self-righteousness was not suitable or sufficient to help me in my time of need. I needed help. I needed sympathy. I needed a Priest. I needed the Jesus perfectly portrayed in the book of Hebrews. Priests essentially do two things: offer sacrifices and make intercession/pray. Hebrews proclaims that Jesus not only sacrificed Himself for sinners, but still prays for His people now.

Hebrews 4:14–16

"Since then we have a great high priest who has passed through the heavens, Jesus, the Son of God, let us hold fast our confession. For we do not have a high priest who is unable to sympathize with our weaknesses, but one who in every respect has been tempted as we are, yet without sin. Let us then with confidence draw near to the throne of grace, that we may receive mercy and find grace to help in time of need."

What comes forth from a "throne of grace?" Answer: grace! When the suffering child of God needs help from One who understands their weaknesses and needs sympathy (not just empathy), Jesus, the Son of God, liberally gives assistance, grace, and mercy in the exact time of their need. What an incredible Priest.

I am certain that having cancer qualifies as a time of need, don't you? And since that is a fact, draw near to Jesus with confidence. By God's grace I did. You can too. Run to Him with boldness. You simply and confidently go to your Savior and the lover of your soul. Just because Jesus has passed through the heavens does not make Him far from or unable to help those He came to rescue. Hebrews and cancer. One showed me my inadequacies and the other showed me my gracious High Priest. Maybe you should read Hebrews today. Why don't you stop reading this book now, lay your burden before the Lord Jesus, and ask for help? If you can't pray, know Jesus is praying for you

CHAPTER 3
INVISIBLE REALITIES

Please read the following verses:

James 1:2–5
"Count it all joy, my brothers, when you meet trials of various kinds, for you know that the testing of your faith produces steadfastness. And let steadfastness have its full effect, that you may be perfect and complete, lacking in nothing. If any of you lacks wisdom, let him ask God, who gives generously to all without reproach, and it will be given him."

Romans 5:1–5
"Therefore, since we have been justified by faith, we have peace with God through our Lord Jesus Christ. Through him we have also obtained access by faith into this grace in which we stand, and we rejoice in hope of the glory of God. Not only that, but we rejoice in our sufferings, knowing that suffering produces endurance, and endurance produces character, and character produces hope, and hope does not put us to shame, because God's love has been poured into our hearts through the Holy Spirit who has been given to us."

What do you notice that is similar in the two passages you just read? I trust you noticed words like: *joy, rejoice, testing, steadfastness, endurance, character,* and *hope*. Whether we realize it or not, the triune God is using trials to mold and shape us into the image of the Lord Jesus. We cannot always see this and that is why this chapter contains the word *invisible*. Perhaps the word *imperceptible* would also work. Like a child feverishly asking his parent, "Am I growing?" only to be shown the pencil marks on the door proving that he is.

Christian with cancer, you know that cancer, left untreated, slowly eats away at your good molecules, good tissues, good blood, and good organs. In a similar, but spiritual and better way, the Holy Spirit Himself is slowly and steadily dealing with the sin in your life. God is even taking cancer and using it to produce a holy character in you and in me. We do not rejoice that we have cancer, but we "count it all joy" and "rejoice" that, even though cancer is an enemy and killer, the Lord of the universe does only what He can: utilize cancer to make us more like Jesus.

It took a long time for me to say these words from my heart, but I finally humbled myself and said them out loud like I meant them: "Lord, I want to sincerely thank you for cancer and for what you are doing through it." Insert tears here. Now it is your turn.

CHAPTER 4
THE DESPERATE CRY OF A HURTING CHRISTIAN

Romans 8:14–17

"For all who are led by the Spirit of God are sons of God. For you did not receive the spirit of slavery to fall back into fear, but you have received the Spirit of adoption as sons, by whom we cry, "Abba! Father!" The Spirit himself bears witness with our spirit that we are children of God, and if children, then heirs—heirs of God and fellow heirs with Christ, provided we suffer with him in order that we may also be glorified with him."

How do you know you are a Christian? There are many evidences that reveal your standing before God, but faith in the risen Jesus is the most important. Romans 8:14-17 shows another way you can know you are saved. Christians, when they are really hurting, call out to God. Sound familiar? Sound like what you did after your diagnosis? The word *cry* in the above Bible passage is not a whimper. It is not muffled or quiet. It is a reflex act that loudly calls out for assistance. Sinclair Ferguson brilliantly explains the idea:

> The picture is not that of the believer resting quietly in his Father's arms in childlike faith, but of the child who has tripped and fallen crying out in pain, "daddy, daddy." That cry is

the mark of the presence of the Spirit of adoption, not least because it shows that in time of need it is towards our Father in heaven that we look.[1]

Christians dealing with cancer, like you, cry out, sometimes loudly and sometimes with a shriek, "Help!" There is nothing wrong with that. Actually, there is everything right with that. In deep and dark trials, you understand that you don't have enough resources of your own to cope, therefore you cry out to the Almighty. Think of a little child who falls and skins her knees on the asphalt. I can hear the wail, "Daddy, help!" Tears.

Hurting Christians call out to God their heavenly Father. With intense focus, believers call out to God. Needy believers, struggling with cancer, know they are needy, and that God their Father has resources, keeps His promises, and hears their prayers. They also know that God loves them. Luther said:

> Although I be oppressed with anguish and terror on every side and seem to be forsaken and utterly cast away from your presence, yet am I your child, and you are my Father for Christ's sake: I am beloved because of a

---

[1] Sinclair Ferguson, The Christian Life (Carlisle: The Banner of Truth Trust, 1981), 100.

Beloved. Wherefore, this little word, "Father," conceived effectually in the heart, passes all the eloquence of Demosthenes.

CHAPTER 5
GOD IS SOVEREIGN OVER YOUR CANCER[2]

The Bible gives clear statements about the extent of God's sovereignty, which includes cancer.

Psalm 103:19
"The LORD has established His throne in the heavens, and His kingdom rules over all."

Psalm 115:3
"Our God is in the heavens; He does all He pleases."

God's sovereign rule knows no boundaries or limits. Charles Hodge said God's sovereignty "can neither be ignored nor rejected. It binds all creatures, as inexorable as physical laws bind the material universe."[3] His control is what people would deem as micro-managing or hands-on, that is, God is involved, not just generally, but also intimately—in all the details. The Scriptures teach that luck, randomness, fate, fortune, happenstance, accidents, and raw chance are nouns not to be used in the King of King's realm.

---

[2] This chapter is taken from my book (with slight modifications), *The Sovereignty and Supremacy of King Jesus* (Leominister: Day One Publications, 2011).

[3] Charles Hodge, *Systematic Theology*, vol. 1 (New York: Scribner, Armstrong, and Co., 1873), 440.

Even the vocabulary of sovereign rule bellows forth the rule of God. When you hear of these biblical words, the idea of total control should rush into your mind: Lord, LORD, Lord of Hosts, Most High, King, Sovereign, Almighty, throne, appointed, established, reign, dominion, rule, decree, ordain, command, predestine, foreordain, authority, and control. Knowledge of this fact is not only the grounds for our trusting in God's future prophecies, but is also the basis for our complete confidence and dependence upon God—for today and the future. Jerry Bridges concurs,

> Confidence in the sovereignty of God in all that affects us is crucial to our trusting Him. If there is a single event in all of the universe that can occur outside of God's sovereign control then we cannot trust Him. His love may be infinite, but if His power is limited and His purpose can be thwarted, we cannot trust Him.[4]

Dear Christian with cancer. God knows. God cares. God can be trusted. While you were taken off guard when you found out your diagnosis, God was not. God is not biting His proverbial fingernails (which He does not have). God is King. God is King over your cancer. Take comfort in the sovereignty of God.

---

[4] Jerry Bridges, *Trusting God: Even When Life Hurts* (Colorado Springs: NavPress, 2008), 37.

CHAPTER 6
HOW CAN I BE A CHRISTIAN SINCE I SIN SO MUCH?[5]

Christians sin. It is a fact. We are to hate it when we sin, but we say it is to be true. Christians believe 1 John:

1 John 1:8–10
"If we say we have no sin, we deceive ourselves, and the truth is not in us. If we confess our sins, he is faithful and just to forgive us our sins and to cleanse us from all unrighteousness. If we say we have not sinned, we make him a liar, and his word is not in us."

Christians, especially those experiencing a severe trial like cancer, do not always respond well to their circumstances. They are weak, frail, and afraid. Again, this is no excuse for their sinning, it is just reality. When Christians sin, they often struggle with the assurance of their salvation. Believers need to be reminded that assurance is both objective and subjective, not simply subjective. Subjective assurance looks to the fruit of faithfulness in the life of the Christian. Spirit-borne fruit is seen and therefore the believer is confirmed in his or her salvation. But objective assurance is the most important aspect of

---

[5] This chapter is taken from my book, *Gospel Assurance: A 31 Day Guide to Assurance.*

assurance. What is objective about it? The object of one's faith is the key. The book of 1 John goes on to give objective assurance:

> **1 John 2:1–2**
> *"My little children, I am writing these things to you so that you may not sin. But if anyone does sin, we have an advocate with the Father, Jesus Christ the righteous. He is the propitiation for our sins, and not for ours only but also for the sins of the whole world."*

May this book direct your attention away from cancer and to the center of the universe, the Advocate Jesus. If you want comfort, balm, and the assurance of your salvation, even when you still struggle spiritually because of cancer, Jesus is the key. If you desire a sure confidence that your sins are forgiven, the Son of Man must be central. The assurance of salvation is never to be divorced from the King of kings, Christ Jesus. What is true for Christian growth is true for Christian assurance. Sinclair Ferguson agrees,

> The ability to focus our gaze, fill our minds, and devote our hearts to Jesus Christ is a basic element in real Christian growth. Inability to do so is a sign of immaturity... They seem to be dominated by feelings, rather than the gospel.

CHAPTER 7
WHAT TO SAY?

All of us have said dumb things to people who are in trials. Have you ever uttered a statement like, "Well, I am sorry you lost your grandmother, but she did live a full life of ninety-four years"? As if that will take away the sting and loss. I digress, but I confess I have said, and still say, stupid things. We want to comfort and soothe, but our well-meaning motives translate into popping the clutch of our mouth and speaking without thinking.

Since we have failed others in this area, let's not be too self-righteous and judge others too harshly. At least they came to visit you when you were sick. By showing up in person, they have obeyed the second greatest commandment, "Love your neighbor as yourself." In this case, let actions speak louder than words. Be thankful. Don't be too hard on them.

One approach might be this: you, yourself can turn the conversation into something that will benefit your visitors spiritually. You can also ask your visitor to read you some Scripture. Sometimes the cancer-targeting drugs, chemotherapy, or long days of being in the infusion room can make it hard to read. "Would you mind reading me Psalm 103 and Psalm 145?" Asking for prayer would also be a prudent option.

How to visit a cancer patient

When you visit a cancer patient, you do not need to say anything. Just show up. Silence, in this circumstance, is not wrong. It is needed. As true as Romans 8:28 is when it says, "And we know that for those who love God all things work together for good, for those who are called according to his purpose," you do not have to quote it. There will be a later time to quote verses like that. Being there is ministry. Being available is loving. Quietness is appropriate. Presence matters. Don't be ashamed to cry with the patient.

Romans 12:15 is clear:
"Rejoice with those who rejoice, weep with those who weep."

At the end of your visit, there is nothing wrong with gently asking, "Can I please pray for you?" And it isn't wrong to ask the person if they would like you to read Scripture, but do not feel like you have to in order to make your visit profitable.

Is there anyone you need to go visit? Go. You don't have to say a word.

CHAPTER 8
REDEEMING BLOOD TESTS

"Do you have an arm preference for the blood draw?" "Please roll up your sleeve." "Make a fist." "We need to take some extra blood for the additional studies." Do I look at the needle going in? The needle gauge seems bigger today. Ouch, a collapsed vein. They go and get the "expert" for round two. Back again tomorrow. Back every day you are at the hospital.

Within about twenty minutes, the results of the blood test arrive in my hospital portal online. "MyChart" gives me such speedy results that I greedily examine them before the doctor and the staff even see them (this is not always a great idea, but I can't help myself. Don't judge, you do it too!). Each test can also be couched in trends, with charts and graphs. I am typically tested for WBC, RBC, HGB, HCT, PLT, MCV, MCH, MCHC, RDW, MPV, NRBC, absolute NRBC, Diff Method, NEUTS, LYMPHS, MONOS, EOS, BASOS, bilirubin direct and more.

Every cancer patient knows this is simply part of the unchanging routine. It is part of the regimen. I am not complaining because the reports yield precious and vital information needed to help the doctors form a game plan for treatment.

One day I asked myself, "Is there any way to redeem this whole process in the lab?" Here is my attempt to help you with "blood draw redemption."

When you get your blood drawn, remind yourself of the Creator. The human body is an amazing creation. The details of blood show how intricately God made us. For example, Regina Bailey comments on some interesting facts about blood:

- The adult human body contains approximately 1.325 gallons of blood.
- Blood makes up about 7 to 8 percent of a person's total body weight.
- The human heart pumps about one million barrels of blood during an average lifetime. That is enough to fill more than three super tankers.
- On average, it takes about forty-five seconds for a single drop of blood to circulate from the heart, all around the body, and back to the heart again.[6]

How could evolution, which involves not a mind or power, figure out how to perfectly make human blood? How much is the right amount? Of what should it be composed? Why should blood

---

[6] Regina Bailey, "Interesting Facts about Blood." Accessed February 2024, available from https://www.thoughtco.com/facts-about-blood-373355; Internet.

contain more than 55 percent plasma? In addition, if blood would be any thinner, people would bleed out over a small cut. If blood was any thicker, the heart could not properly pump it through the body. Blood is what some people call an "irreducible minimum." Evolution has no explanation for blood. So, when I get my blood tests, I try to praise the Lord for how He designed the human body.

In Psalm 139, David extols the Creator. Next time you are in the laboratory waiting room, try reading this Psalm (especially verses 13–18):

> *For you formed my inward parts;*
> *you knitted me together in my mother's womb.*
> *I praise you, for I am fearfully and wonderfully made.*
> *Wonderful are your works;*
> *my soul knows it very well.*
> *My frame was not hidden from you,*
> *when I was being made in secret,*
> *intricately woven in the depths of the earth.*
> *Your eyes saw my unformed substance;*
> *in your book were written, every one of them,*
> *the days that were formed for me,*
> *when as yet there was none of them.*
>
> *How precious to me are your thoughts, O God!*
> *How vast is the sum of them!*
> *If I would count them, they are more than the sand.*
> *I awake, and I am still with you.*

CHAPTER 9
WHAT ABOUT THE FUTURE?

Short term

Every cancer patient thinks about the future. They ask questions like:

- Will the drugs work?
- Is my doctor really the best?
- How much of a future will I actually have?
- Will my quality of life decrease?
- Will there be long-term side effects from the chemotherapy?

Every one of these is appropriate and normal. The hard part is to keep thinking about the long term.

Long term

You will not have cancer forever. In the long term, do not forgot two important events. Both events are guaranteed to happen. The first event is the return of the Lord Jesus, and the second event is the glorification of your body.

The return of the Lord Jesus Christ

There is nothing wrong with wanting Jesus to return, even if you want Him to come back because that would take care of your cancer forever. Do not feel guilty about that. Jesus will come back to make all wrongs right, including sickness, sin, disease, pain, and more.

Read the following verses to remind yourself of the certain return of your Savior. He is coming back for you because He loves you and He has promised it!

John 14:1-6
"Let not your hearts be troubled. Believe in God; believe also in me. In my Father's house are many rooms. If it were not so, would I have told you that I go to prepare a place for you? And if I go and prepare a place for you, I will come again and will take you to myself, that where I am you may be also. And you know the way to where I am going." Thomas said to him, "Lord, we do not know where you are going. How can we know the way?" Jesus said to him, "I am the way, and the truth, and the life. No one comes to the Father except through me."

The glorification of your body

The other aspect of long-term thinking is regarding your body. You will get a new body one day and it will be perfect, impervious to cancer and every sickness. Since that is true, what does Paul say to do here?

> ### 2 Corinthians 4:16–18
> *"So we do not lose heart. Though our outer self is wasting away, our inner self is being renewed day by day. For this light momentary affliction is preparing for us an eternal weight of glory beyond all comparison, as we look not to the things that are seen but to the things that are unseen. For the things that are seen are transient, but the things that are unseen are eternal."*

My father used to say, "stinkin' thinkin'" often. Might I suggest that stinking thinking is simply living in the present without an eye to the future?

CHAPTER 10
IT IS GOOD TO FEAR

We fear when we have cancer. But we fear the wrong things, like:

- Fear regarding the next blood test
- Fear of having to tell your family of your disease worsening
- Fear of the unknown
- Fear that the cancer will come back
- Fear that your spouse will be widowed (or become a widower)
- Fear of the children losing a parent
- Fear of not walking your daughter down the aisle at her wedding
- Fear of missing out on grandchildren
- Fear of judgment
- Fear of hearing the words, "terminal," or "Stage 4"

Instead of fearing the above, we need to replace those unhelpful and unproductive fears with a godly fear. Is there a godly fear? Yes. And you probably know this common refrain from the Bible, "The fear of the Lord is the beginning of wisdom."

Patients rightly need to become their own best health care advocate. Empowered by the availability of information about cancer and the best doctors, people with cancer are no longer ignorant or lacking information about their disease. But sometimes, while knowledgeable, they are unwise. Sometimes I am unwise. The great news is that we do not have to stay that way.

The Bible is clear about wisdom:

Psalm 111:10
"The fear of the LORD is the beginning of wisdom; all those who practice it have a good understanding. His praise endures forever!"

"The fear of the LORD." What does it mean? How can a proper understanding of it help me in the middle of chemotherapy, infusions, biopsies, and surgery? Here is the key: the "fear of the LORD" is different based on your relationship to the God who made the universe and who made you. Let's start with the unbeliever first. For them "fear" is actually fear.

Hebrews 10:31
"It is a fearful thing to fall into the hands of the living God."

Because of their sins against a thrice-holy God, unbelievers should shake in horror of the prospect of meeting God on Judgment Day. They should tremble. They should be afraid. If you are an unbeliever,

Luther said you should have a "servile fear." Such fear is that of a slave. A slave crouching. A fear of the tormenter.

For the Christian, because of the work of the triune God, his or her position is that of son or daughter. Therefore, instead of a servile fear is what Luther termed a "filial fear." *Filial* means "son." To an earthly son or daughter, their earthly father is not a judge. For a Christian, all of God's judgment has been poured out on the Son. Jesus totally assuaged the wrath of God. Jesus made propitiation for all of God's holy wrath. Jesus drank the entire cup of judgment. Christians therefore have nothing for which to be judged. When Jesus said on Calvary, "It is finished," the work was accomplished, paid in full.

Think of fear this way: your heavenly Father is so great, powerful, awesome, and loving, that you want to honor Him, make Him look good, and obey Him. You want this not so you can become a son or daughter, but because you already are a son or daughter. A healthy respect and awe is due Him.

Now, dear suffering Christian, replace the fear of cancer with the fear of the Lord.

CHAPTER 11
YOU HAVE A MINISTRY

When I found out I had cancer for the first time, someone, in a roundabout manner said, "Mike, God gave you a ministry." I thought, "I already have a ministry, I am the pastor at a local church." The person meant, "You have a ministry to people with cancer." My mind said silently, "But I never signed up for it." It is true for all of us, we did not ask for cancer, and we never signed up for cancer or a cancer ministry. But we now have a unique opportunity to help other people with cancer because we know exactly what it feels like. We know the emotions, talks with the family, innumerable doctor visits, ups, downs, prayers, tears, and more.

Dear Christian with cancer: like it or not, you have a ministry to others. I want to talk about two areas of your new ministry.

To others with cancer

The Apostle Paul is clear in his introductory praise in the book of 2 Corinthians. While even Peter said some of Paul's writings were difficult to understand, this passage in 2 Corinthians is straightforward and simple:

2 Corinthians 1:3–6

"Blessed be the God and Father of our Lord Jesus Christ, the Father of mercies and God of all comfort, who comforts us in all our affliction, so that we may be able to comfort those who are in any affliction, with the comfort with which we ourselves are comforted by God."

Did you notice all the names of God listed in the above blessing? "God and Father of our Lord Jesus Christ," "Father of mercies," and "God of all comfort." What names. What love. What comfort. Far from being a God who is far away and reluctant to help, the Lord is close to His children and always ready to assist in every trial we go through, including cancer.

Now comes the ministry part. Paul goes on to write that Christians end up being conduits of God's comfort. We pass along God's comfort. It works like this: God comforts us, and we then comfort others.

To the hospital/clinic's staff

While captive to a ten-hour IV infusion, I had many opportunities to be kind to the staff and on occasion preach the gospel. The same goes for you. Martin Holdt was a wonderful Christian pastor in South Africa. I once said to him in Johannesburg, "I wish you were my father." His kindness and evangelistic zeal were infectious. He had a habit of going up to people, regardless of their ethnicity or station in life, and asking with a smile, "Have you read your Bible today?" One day in the cancer hospital, after getting to know my nurse for the day, I asked the Martin Holdt question. She said, "No," and responded with a guilty look. We had a good conversation about it. It ended with me smiling and saying, "It isn't too late to start reading your Bible. You will find wonderful things in it about Jesus Christ."

Remember, you have a ministry! You can always say, "How can I pray for you?"

CHAPTER 12
DOES GOD STILL LOVE ME?

Sometimes sick people think bad thoughts. While sickness is never an excuse for sin or ungodly thinking, we all know it is harder to obey when you do not feel well. Again, we are not justifying sin, we are simply granting that we are weak and frail people. I am not sure if these kinds of wrong thoughts have ever entered your mind or not? It goes like this,

"In light of my cancer diagnosis,"
"Does God love me?"
"Did God stop loving me?"
"Maybe my sinful response to cancer has changed God's mind about me?"
"Has my relationship with the Lord changed?"

Dear suffering Christian, God still loves you. As a matter of fact, He never started to love you because He has always loved you, even in eternity. And therefore, God will NEVER stop loving you.

Speaking of eternity past, that is a forgotten place to go when thinking about the love of God. It might be hard to think of eternity, but the payoff is marvelous. Of course, the love of God was put on full display at the Cross, but that is not the only place to see God's love. Actually, when you contemplate eternity and the agreement within the Trinity to save sinners, Calvary is better understood and more appreciated. The salvation we have as Christians was planned before the world was created. Our salvation was not random nor was it lucky. Jesus came into this world to save sinners and fulfill His mission. What does the Father sending the Son teach you about God's love? Paul concludes Romans 8 with more questions about God's love. And answers. The questions in Romans 8 also answer more questions like:

- Does God love Christians with cancer?
- Will God love me even if I die from cancer?
- Will cancer separate me from the love of God?
- If my love for God fails and falters, will God's love for me fail and falter?

Romans 8:35, 37–39

"Who shall separate us from the love of Christ? Shall tribulation, or distress, or persecution, or famine, or nakedness, or danger, or sword? No, in all these things we are more than conquerors through him who loved us. For I am sure that neither death nor life, nor angels nor rulers, nor things present nor things to come, nor powers, nor height nor depth, nor anything else in all creation, will be able to separate us from the love of God in Christ Jesus our Lord."

After reading those verses, we no longer need to ask questions about God's love.

CHAPTER 13
JESUS KNOWS ABOUT SUFFERING

The incarnation of Jesus Christ is important in so many ways. The eternal Son needed to be perfectly man so He could be both man's representative and substitute. While Jesus never suffered from cancer, He did suffer. And truth be told, what Jesus suffered makes cancer look like a temporary blip on the radar screen. Hebrews 2 crystalizes all these truths and more.

Hebrews 2:14–18
"Since therefore the children share in flesh and blood, he himself likewise partook of the same things, that through death he might destroy the one who has the power of death, that is, the devil, and deliver all those who through fear of death were subject to lifelong slavery. For surely it is not angels that he helps, but he helps the offspring of Abraham. Therefore he had to be made like his brothers in every respect, so that he might become a merciful and faithful high priest in the service of God, to make propitiation for the sins of the people. For because he himself has suffered when tempted, he is able to help those who are being tempted."

Cancer patient, or cancer survivor, Jesus knows about suffering. Jesus actually suffered during His whole life on earth. Satanic temptations, betrayal, arrest, and more punctuated His time here. The

Heidelberg Catechism, Question 37 asks, "What do you understand by the word 'suffered'"? The answer:

> That all the time He lived on earth, but especially at the end of His life, He bore, in body and soul, the wrath of God against the sin of the whole human race; in order that by His passion, as the only atoning sacrifice, He might redeem our body and soul from everlasting damnation, and obtain for us the grace of God, righteousness and eternal life.

Issac Watts' poem, "Why Did Christ Suffer?" serves as an appropriate way to end this chapter about Christ's suffering. It will remind you of the Great High Priest's love for you. It will gladden your heart that God is not aloof, far off, or unable to understand or help His children.

> Jesus, my great High Priest,
> Offered his blood and died;
> My guilty conscience seeks
> No sacrifice beside.
> His pow'rful blood did once atone,
> And now it pleads before the throne.[7]

---

[7] Issac Watts, "Jesus My Great High Priest," from Trinity Hymnal, ref. ed., (Suwanee, GA: Great Commission Publications, 1990), selection 306.

CHAPTER 14
"IT IS THE MEDICINE"

Every pastor needs a pastor. My pastor is a man named Phil Howard. I do not know the exact numbers, but I am sure he has pastored for over fifty years and has been married for over sixty years. He is retired from full time ministry, but regularly preaches and teaches the Word, with a special focus on extolling the Lord Jesus Christ. He also regularly gives sage advice to young bucks like me.

When I told Pastor Phil of my leukemia diagnosis in the fall of 2023, he listened, cared, and showed his trademark compassion to me. Phil has experienced his own share of extreme trials, so he is extra sympathetic and keen to help. I do not remember a lot of details of the conversation, since I was still trying to process my treatment, prognosis, and more, but I distinctly recall four words that seemed to bellow through a megaphone: *It. Is. The. Medicine.*

What did Phil say before those four words? He wanted me to know that cancer-targeting drugs, infusion therapy, radiation, and chemotherapy can, and will, affect a person. Obviously, there is a physical element to the drugs. I have headaches (the doctor said to drink more coffee to offset the headaches. I love that except I like to sleep. I am also extremely tired, have major GI issues [I will spare you the details], and sleep is sometimes not very restful).

Yet, there are more side effects of the medicine. Besides being lethargic, I can become emotional, cry for no real reason, and really struggle to have joy. It is like my joy or happiness meter is on hold. I certainly LOVE to see my grandchildren, have a nice meal with my wife, do some winter skiing and get on the bicycle for a joy ride. My grown children and the spouses of my children are all wonderful. But something with me is "off." I am not clinically depressed, and I am not making excuses for my behavior if/when I sin. While it might be easier to sin on certain medicines, like it might be easier to sin if someone's hormones were messed up, or a person had a migraine, sin cannot ultimately be blamed on anything but the person sinning.

Here comes the proverbial "but." But, as Phil said, "It is the medicine." In other words, my friend wanted me to know that some of the things I feel and think do not make me a carnal person. They are not relegating me to "walking by the flesh." Christian, let me be Pastor Phil to you and boldly say: The medicines you are taking are powerful and will affect more than your body. Your emotional roller coaster rides will one day end after your treatment. Don't get down on yourself and figure that you must be "backsliding."

Rest, by faith, in your risen Savior. Be thankful. Strive for holiness. Pray. Repent. Confess. But DO NOT blame everything that you are feeling on sinful thinking or carnal living. You are sick. You have cancer. You are a whole person, body, soul, emotions, will, and more. The intense cancer medicines take their toll on your immune system, your blood, your liver, your kidneys, and your emotional state.

Remember, especially in your down-in-the-dark-valley days, four simple words:

It is the medicine.

CHAPTER 15
YOU CAN TRUST YOUR HEAVENLY FATHER, SO DON'T WORRY

Do you ever worry? Are you ever anxious? Sadly, I have never worried more in my life than I have over cancer. I have lost two grandparents and both parents to cancer. I have had two different types of cancer. Maybe you can identify with me, especially in those moments in the middle of the night. The boa constrictor of worry starts to suffocate you and the worries exponentially multiply. The English word for worry comes from a word that means, "to strangle," or grasp by the throat.

What do you think God's attitude is about worry? While we compartmentalize worry and exclude it from grave sins such as adultery and murder, worry is still sin against the Lord. Worry functionally questions the sovereignty of God, God's faithfulness, and the Lord's provision for His children. Dear Christian with cancer, God does not want you to worry. For your sake. And His glory. Consider it the ABCs of dealing with worry.

A. Admit anxiety and worry are sins.

Gulp. If Jesus tells you not to do something, but you do it anyway, what is that called? It is called, "sin."

Matthew 6:25

"Therefore I tell you, do not be anxious about your life, what you will eat or what you will drink, nor about your body, what you will put on. Is not life more than food, and the body more than clothing?"

There is hope when you confess sin. It is forgiven and you receive mercy. Proverbs 28:13 confirms this fact, "Whoever conceals his transgressions will not prosper, but he who confesses and forsakes them will obtain mercy." If you label your sin as a "disease," "syndrome," or "illness," there will be no mercy. You want mercy, right? Why don't you confess your anxiety right now? Yes, even about your cancer.

B. Believe your heavenly Father is loving, good, and provides for all your needs.

Matthew 6:26

"Look at the birds of the air: they neither sow nor reap nor gather into barns, and yet your heavenly Father feeds them. Are you not of more value than they?"

Jesus said, "look." He commands His followers to consider, gaze up, and intently stare with serious contemplation. "Be a bird watcher." But there is more, "Watch birds and then consider what the Father does for them." Birds have food from God. Will God feed us and provide for us? The argument is from the lesser to the greater. Martin Luther is wise in his analysis:

> You see, he is making the birds our schoolmasters and teachers. It is a great and abiding disgrace to us that in the gospel a helpless sparrow should become a theologian and a preacher to the wisest of men.[8]

Jesus calls his disciples to "consider" a second time.

Matthew 6:28-29
"And why are you anxious about clothing? Consider the lilies of the field, how they grow: they neither toil nor spin, yet I tell you, even Solomon in all his glory was not arrayed like one of these."

The Greek word is different here, instead of consider by intently gazing, it means to consider by careful study or observation. So many Christians operate on their feelings. Cancer sufferers need to think. They need to consider. They need to contemplate their heavenly Father who loves them.

C. Chase after God and His glory

---

[8] Martin Luther, *Luther's Works, Vol 21: The Sermon on the Mount* (St. Louis: Concordia Press, 1956), 197-98.

Please do not let worry handicap your worship of the Lord today. Do not let anxiety sidetrack you from serving Jesus Christ and His church. Jesus said,

Matthew 6:33
"But seek first the kingdom of God and his righteousness, and all these things will be added to you."

Seeking requires deliberate searching with strenuous effort. Jesus wants you to constantly seek His kingdom. Instead of constantly seeking Google remedies, life expectancies, herbal cures, and more, strive for God's kingdom and righteousness. Live "all out" for the Lord. Be so busy serving the Lord and other Christians that you do not have time to worry.

D. Do not borrow trouble

I admit that much of my worry related to cancer has nothing to do with today. My worry is often about future procedures, tests, biopsies, infusions, and long-term prognosis. Future worry is not only sinful but unproductive. It accomplishes nothing profitable. The Lord gives grace for today, but He does not give tomorrow's grace for today.

Matthew 6:34
"Therefore do not be anxious about tomorrow, for tomorrow will be anxious for itself. Sufficient for the day is its own trouble."

Overcoming worry about cancer is as simple as the ABCs. Or in this case, the ABCDs. Why don't you go outside for a walk and watch the birds and look at the blossoms. If you are too sick to walk, go sit by your favorite window and observe God the Father's care over fowls and flowers.

Made in the USA
Middletown, DE
06 January 2025